To

_____

From

_____

Published by Hallmark Gift Books,
a division of Hallmark Cards, Inc.,
Kansas City, MO 64141
Visit us on the Web at Hallmark.com.

Editorial Director: Delia Berrigan
Editors: Amber Stenger and Chelsea Fogleman Resnick
Art Director: Chris Opheim
Designer: Mary Eakin
Production Artist: Bryan Ring
Photo Retoucher: Greg Ham

ISBN: 978-1-59530-540-4
SKU: 1BOK1218

Made in China
1117

Dreams for My
Daughter

A Mother's Lifetime of Hopes Come True

By Ellen Brenneman

Hallmark
gift books

Daughter,

I've always had so many dreams for you . . .

It all started even before I knew for sure there was going to be a "you."

I just had this feeling that I wanted to be a mom and had a big comfy chair all picked out where I'd rock you and give you all the hugs you could ever need.

I couldn't wait to see you, to hold you
in my arms, to count your tiny toes . . .

and to wrap you up in a soft, fluffy blanket.

Your sleepy little sighs
were my new favorite sound,
better than any song I'd ever liked . . .

and your sweet little expressions
as you explored your world
became my new favorite show.

I dreamed that even from your first steps, you'd have a feeling that the whole world was yours and you could go anywhere and do anything—

that no limits would ever hold you back.

I wanted you to experience the world

as safe and good, big, welcoming, and beautiful . . .

with a place for you wherever you
chose to fly.

Some of the most memorable times
were those toddler days
when you started showing
you had a mind and personality of your own . . .

your little face covered in **PB&J**,
your determined pout,
the outfits you came up with
when you insisted on dressing yourself!

I hoped and dreamed
that your personality would be shaped
by a sense of confidence . . .

an assurance that no matter what, you'd be loved and supported for being you.

I hoped, too, that I'd give you just enough guidance
and just enough of your own space in the sun

so you'd **really blossom** in your own way . . .

with that independent spirit that was always so "you" and that smile that just seemed to bubble up from your happy heart.

I loved watching you learn new things.
With each accomplishment,
I saw a spark in your eyes
growing brighter and brighter.

Letting go of your little hand for the first time
and watching you go off by yourself
left me with a little lump in my throat
(**OK**, a big one)
and an even bigger sense of pride.

I dreamed that you'd make friends easily,
that you'd pick good examples to pattern yourself
after, and that you'd quickly hold your own
in every new environment you faced.

Turns out, I needn't have worried . . .
you were a natural
and surprised even me
with your newfound independence
and big-girl sophistication.

I dreamed that your teachers would give you an awareness of just how open the world was to you and just how much you could achieve, so that you'd feel confident, excited, and soon start dreaming for yourself.

But I also dreamed that you'd have fun along
the way and you'd never lose that sense of
discovery, wonder, and joy
in just being "you" in the world.

I hoped you'd get a few good traits from me
but also develop your own strengths
as you grew into your own person.

I didn't have to wait long
to see that coming true in awesome
and wonderful ways.

Somehow I always knew the world would
see you the same way I did—

as a bright, capable, and unique person made of pretty good stuff inside and out.

I hoped you'd know
I'd always be there for you
with a hug, a warm plate of cookies,
a listening ear,
and, yes, a little motherly advice
(**OK**, **OK** . . . sometimes a lot).

But as you continued
to demonstrate your strengths
and growing wisdom,
I started confidently
letting you take more of the driver's seat
in planning your life.

And it turned out—you make a
pretty good boss of your life.

I dreamed that you'd find a real passion in life—
maybe several—so that your work
wouldn't be "just a job," or even just a career,
but a calling.

I wanted you to have a **sense of fulfillment**
that came from deep within . . .

so that your happiness wouldn't depend on others
or on daily ups and downs

but would come from knowing yourself
and being 100 percent satisfied with who you were.

I wanted the same thing for you when it came to friendships and love . . .

that wonderful people would come
into your life, treat your heart with care,
and give you the kind of love that was
selfless, sustaining, and real.

Even more than that, **I** always hoped
you'd love yourself as much as you
deserved to be loved.

I always knew the paths you chose to pursue might be different from mine— but I also knew you had what it took to make good decisions for yourself.

As you came into your own,
some of the ways you're different from me
turned out to be my favorite things
about you! Who would have predicted that?

And now comes the best part of having
a daughter like you—the fact that we're not just
mother and daughter, but friends, too.

I don't just share my wisdom and advice with you . . .
you share yours with me, too.

I look forward to hearing your perspective on things based on experiences you've had.

I'd think you were pretty smart
(not to mention cool, fun, and wonderful)
even if you weren't my daughter.

In fact, **I** have two big comfy chairs all picked out
where we'll laugh and talk and share stories
some summer afternoon when we're way older
and even better at this friend thing.

Now that so many of the dreams I've always
had for you have come true, I just have one more,
and it's really simple:

May every dream you have in your heart— for yourself, for your life, or for your own family— come true . . .

the big ones, the small ones, the silly ones,
the secret ones you haven't said out loud,
and even the ones you haven't dreamed yet.

A mom can't help having dreams for her daughter, and one of the greatest gifts in my life has been seeing so many of them come true.

You've brought me so many smiles,
so much pride, and so many moments when
I could hardly believe how blessed I've been.

I love being your mom even more than I dreamed . . .
and I love you.

If you have enjoyed this book
or it has touched your life in some way,
we would love to hear from you.

Please send your comments to:
Hallmark Book Feedback
P.O. Box 419034
Mail Drop 215
Kansas City, MO 64141

Or e-mail us at:
booknotes@hallmark.com